Merry Christmas

Jessamine

2016

Love from Grandma

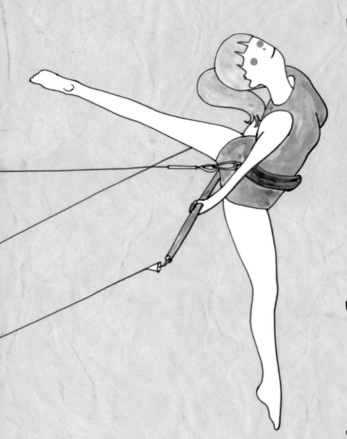

How I Learned to Fly

By Janice Martin

Illustrated by Catalina Nistor

Published by
Flying J Productions, Inc.
www.FlyingJProductions.com

Copyright 2014

ISBN: 978-0-578-14514-3

www.janicemartin.com

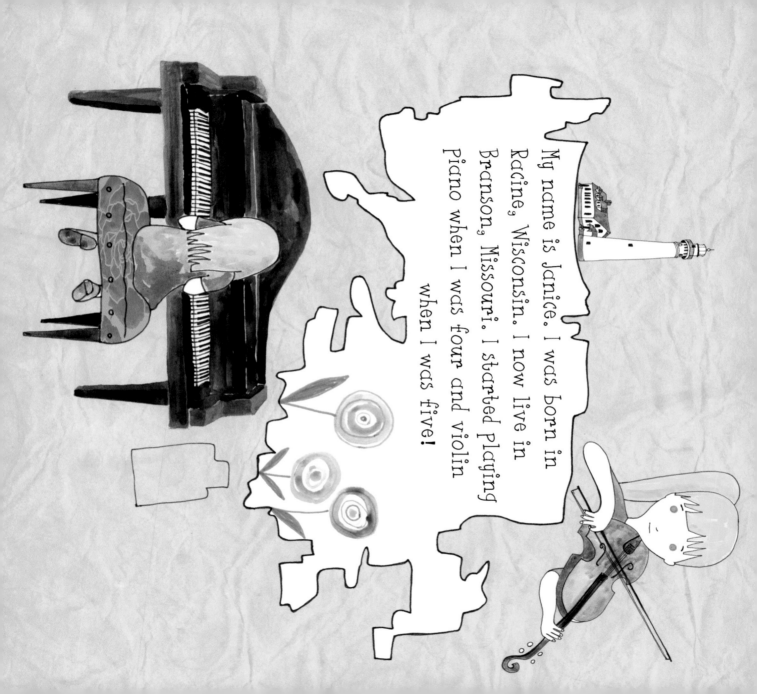

My name is Janice. I was born in Racine, Wisconsin. I now live in Branson, Missouri. I started playing Piano when I was four and violin when I was five!

I grew up the youngest of 3 sisters. To me, my two older sisters were beautiful, strong and courageous. My sisters could climb trees but I could never climb as high as they could.

That made me so upset!

One day, I watched the movie Mary Poppins[66], and I was so excited! I wanted to FLY! I figured that the whole secret to flying, and not being afraid, was to have an umbrella. One afternoon, I found the biggest umbrella we had.

Then when my parents weren't looking, I jumped off the big railing we had on a porch that was very high off the ground!

The umbrella didn't work! I fell straight to the ground and, OUCH, sprained my arm!

I began taking gymnastics when I was eight years old. My favorite apparatus was the uneven bars because they made me feel like I was flying through the air.

I loved to watch the older girls as they glided up and around the bars.

One time, when I was all by myself, I forgot to listen to the rules. I thought I'd get up on a high bar and swing my body around and around like I saw the older gymnasts do. There was no one spotting me and I didn't really know what I was doing. Before I knew it, I was flat on the ground with the wind knocked out of me!

I started falling all the time! I sprained my arm, again, by falling off monkey bars on a playground.

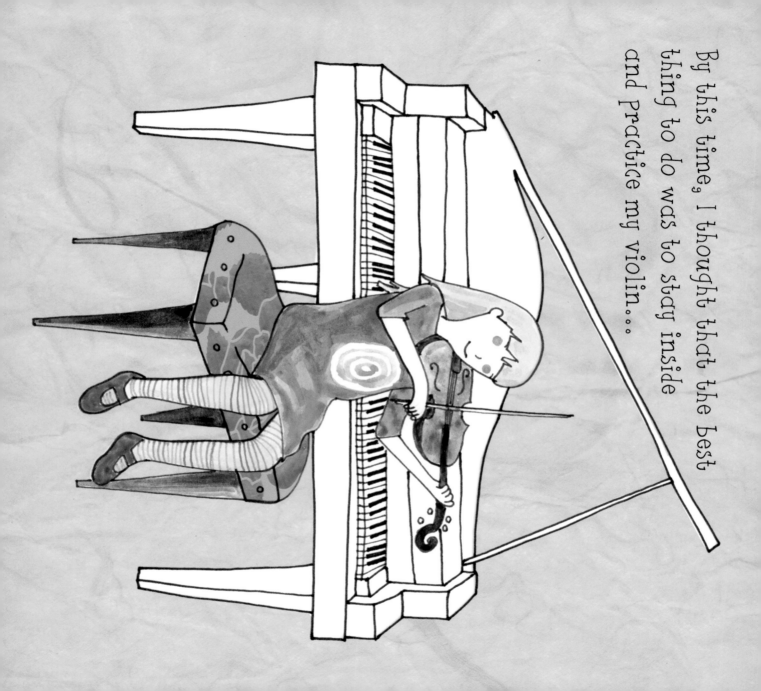

By this time, I thought that the best thing to do was to stay inside and practice my violin...

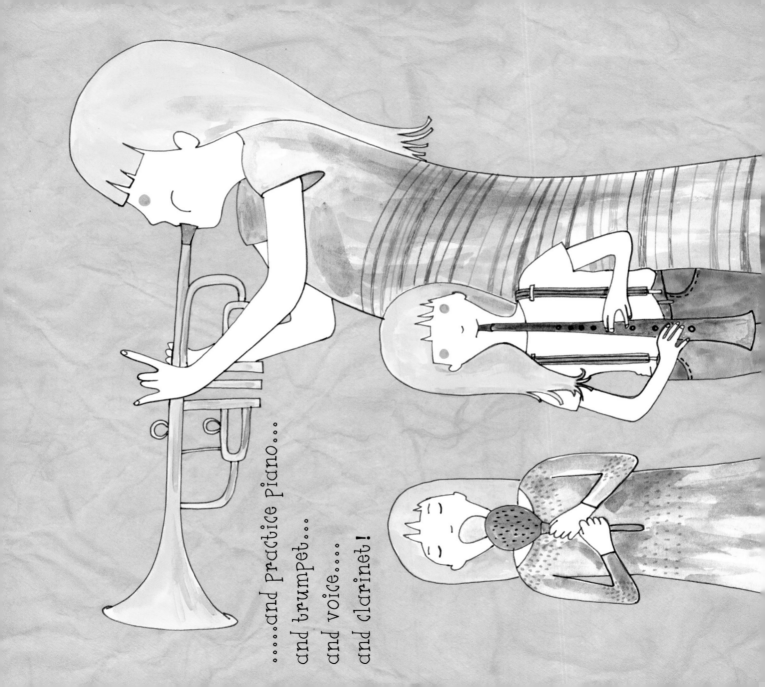

.....and practice piano....
and trumpet....
and voice....
and clarinet!

I was accepted to a great music school called The Juilliard School of Music. I was thrilled because Juilliard is located in New York City, and it is one of the most famous music schools in the world.

I practiced and practiced, so much that I majored in violin performance when I went to college.

The Juilliard School

Our class did a
special concert tour
in France. We
performed in a
cathedral that had
a huge tower!
I was too scared to
climb the stairs to
the top of the tower,
My hands turned
clammy, my knees
shook, and my
stomach turned
over and over!

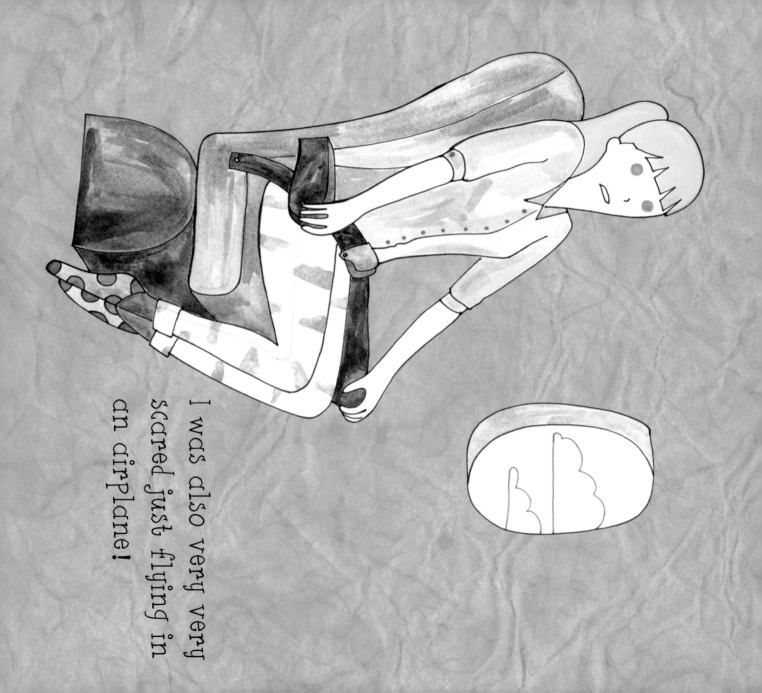

I was also very very scared just flying in an airplane!

I admired my friends who loved to climb, but I was NOT going to try again. I was too afraid!

After studying music I decided to join the United
States Army. I auditioned for the United States
Army Band that performs at The White House for
the President, the Senators and Congressmen.
This is where important meetings are held and
world leaders gather. It was very exciting for me!
They told me I had to go to Basic Training before
I could play in the United States Army Band
because all Army personnel - even the musicians -
need to be trained as soldiers!

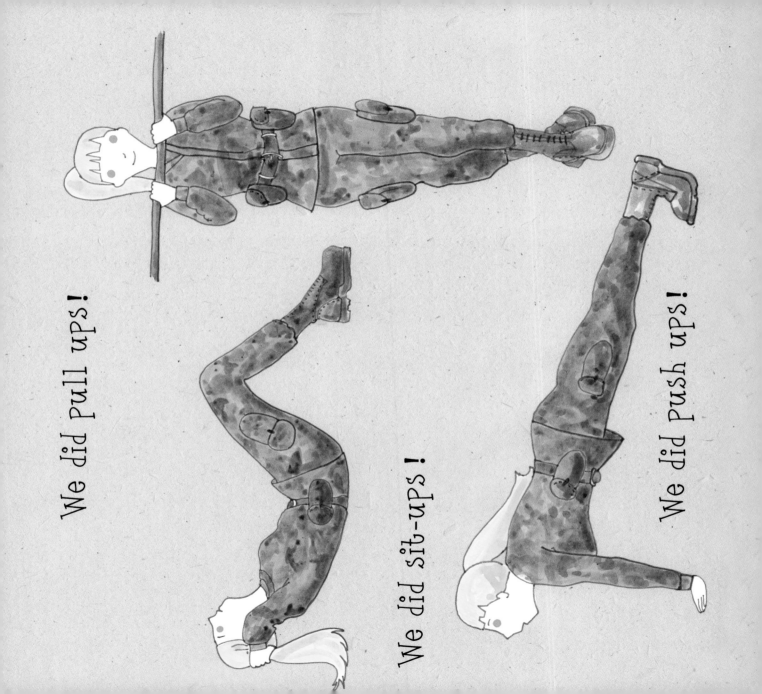

I loved being able to run because it was like flying except I stayed on the ground.

The Drill Sergeant let me run circles around the other soldiers!

One day I was chosen to run in a big race representing my team. I ran as fast as I could and I won the race! But, I ran so fast I pulled a muscle in my leg!

Every day the drill sergeants told us about the Confidence Course. We didn't know what that meant, but every time they talked about it, they sounded like we should be afraid of it!

Finally, near the end of our eight weeks of basic training, they told us it was time for the Confidence Course. We were all very nervous when the Sergeants instructed us to start marching. They said to keep marching until they told us to stop!

A whole field with scary training exercises, the worst of all being a huge 30 foot tower that we were going to have to climb! It towered over our heads like a giant skyscraper!!!

We saw it looming from distance. We marched and marched until... THERE IT WAS!

My leg still hurt
from the race but
I managed to get
through the belly
crawl, the wall
climb, and many
more.

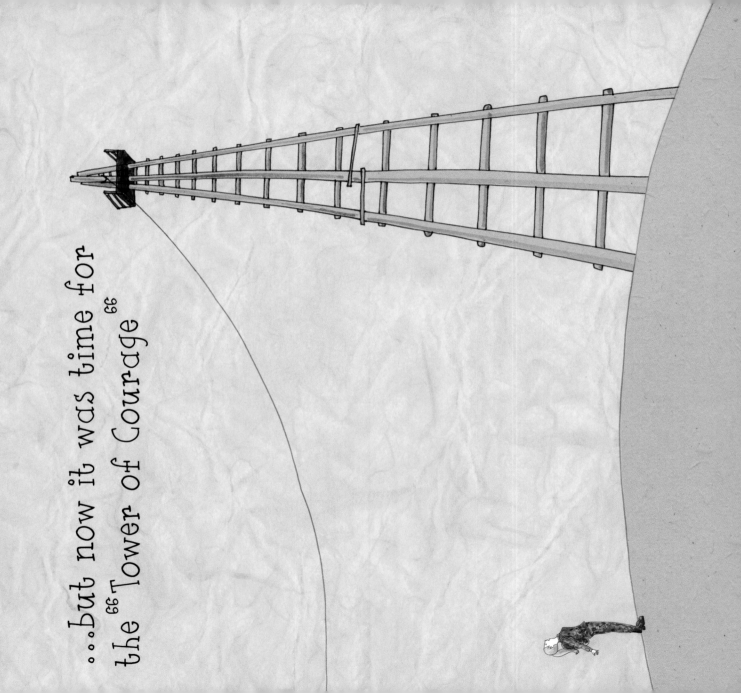

...but now it was time for
the "Tower of Courage"

We were required to wear really heavy things: heavy boots, heavy canteens filled with water, a heavy backpack and a heavy helmet. Plus, my leg was injured! How was I going to do it?

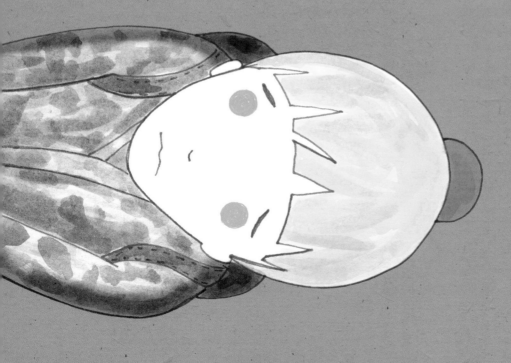

I looked at the drill sergeant who pointed towards the tower. He saw me hesitate and yelled at me to "Get going!" What was I going to do? I COULDN'T get out of this! I HAD to climb!

I was so terrified that my hands started to sweat, my legs started shaking, and my stomach turned over and over. I felt I was going to be sick!

I placed my hand on the ladder forcing myself to climb one step at a time...

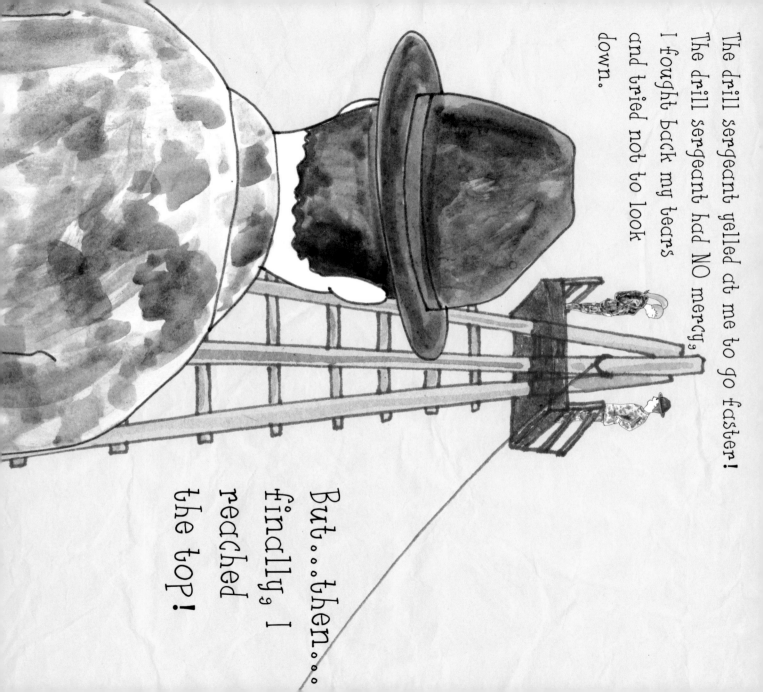

The drill sergeant yelled at me to go faster!
The drill sergeant had NO mercy,
I fought back my tears
and tried not to look
down.

But...then...
finally, I
reached
the top!

There was a drill sergeant stationed at the top. He told me to hoist my legs up and around the rope and slide down to the ground. He gave me the count down, but I stood there paralyzed! How was I going to do this? I was certain I would never survive! How could I lift my feet with heavy boots up to the rope and not lose my GRIP and fall!

The drill sergeant screamed, "ONE, TWO, THREE.... JUMP!"

I don't remember how I did it, but I threw my legs up and grabbed on for dear life... I SLID ALL THE WAY DOWN THE ROPE TO THE GROUND!

I stood dazed at the bottom of the rope until the drill sergeant called out, "All right, Martin! Good job!" Then....I started to smile.

The happiness overtook me! I couldn't believe it!

I DID IT! I DID IT! I DID IT!

That day changed my life! I had just done something I thought I could NEVER do. I had been scared, but I DID IT ANYWAY!

No wonder it was called a Confidence Course! By accomplishing something that I was afraid to do, I had CREATED Confidence in myself!!!

I had CREATED COURAGE!!!

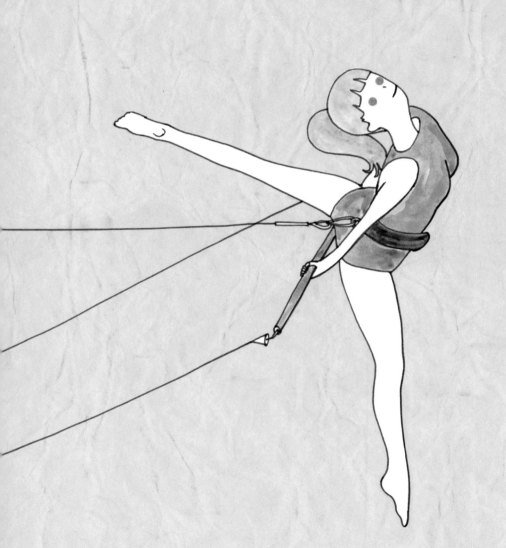

Now that I had conquered my fear of heights,

I decided to GO FOR IT.

I always wanted to fly so I decided to do just that, to learn how to fly through the air on a trapeze!

I was learning all about Circus Aerial Arts and I wanted to try everything. I took lessons on the Aerial Silks and loved them, even though they proved much more difficult than a trapeze.

After three years in the Army, I decided to make a show of my own.

I wanted to create a show that was beautiful and something that no one had ever done before!

I wanted to be the world's ONLY FLYING VIOLINIST!

I practiced every day.
I was invited to perform on television!

I was invited to perform with major orchestras like the Philadelphia Orchestra!

I practiced everywhere
— in the gym, even in
the backyard tied
to a tree.

All my hard work made
my dream come true!
I get invited all over
to perform on
beautiful stages
and share with
audiences all
my talents:

Singing,
Playing violin,
Playing
Piano, and
of course,
flying in
the air
with my
violin!

From the Author:

This is my first attempt at a book, and I feel very grateful for all those who have contributed to it! First I want to thank Catalina Nistor for her brilliance, vision and dedication to making my images come to life in her beautiful illustrations. Second I want to thank Donna Seim for her insights and encouragement in bringing my story to the page. Thank you, my wonderful Zachariah for your support, mechanical expertise and aerial rigging skills by putting up my silks in your back yard using your truck and tractor to help me practice! Thank you Jordann Baker Skipper for your encouragement and guidance in being an aerialist, and of course thank you to my sisters, my mom and my dad for continuing to be a huge inspiration in my life. I love all of you!

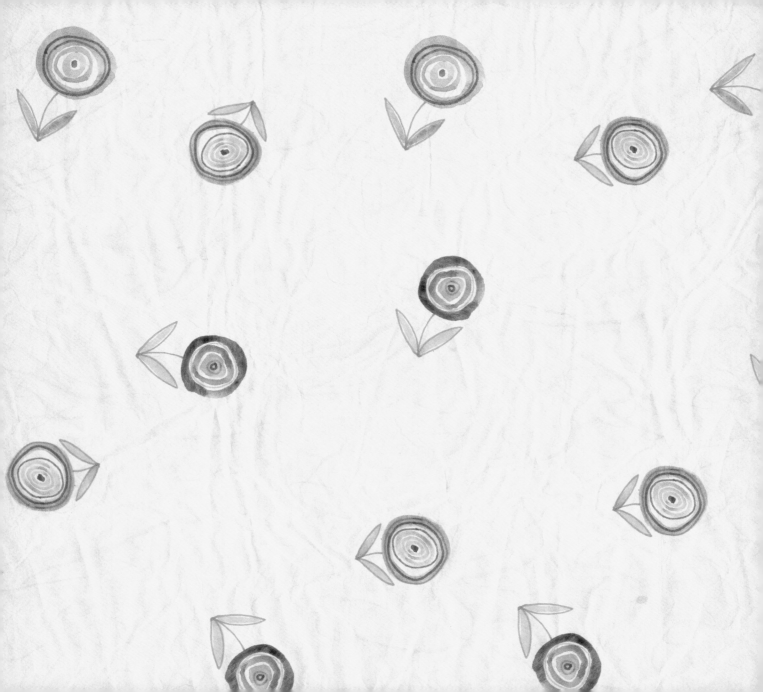